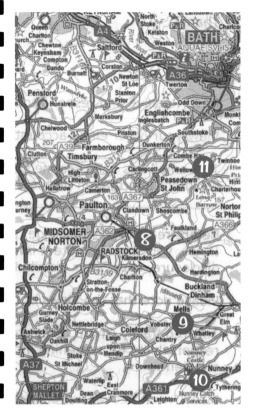

G000292521

Seriously Not Boring
Walks Book
by Sue Gearing and Les Davies

with illustrations by Neil Ross

What's special about this book?

We hope that the **Seriously *NOT* Boring Walks Book** will show you that country walking can be 'wicked' – and certainly not boring!

Here are 12 short circles on and around the Mendip Hills in Somerset, between 3-6km (1.8-3.75 miles) in length.

They are not just ordinary walks – but exploring with fun things to do, such as making a compass in a puddle, flying a kite, building a small shelter, and finding the age of a tree.

So come with us now and join Tom, Mia, Kate, Sam, Harry and the inseparable Scamp, the dog, on 12 circular walks of discovery and adventure for you and your family.

Sue and Les

Before you start, look at the Activities on pages 50-55.

WALK 1 • **A circle out to Sand Point and Middle Hope** • **3.2km** • **Can easily be shortened or lengthened** • **A steep climb up steps to start and a short climb later on, and then only gentle ups and downs** • **The route out to Sand Point is rocky in parts and it is steep on each side so care is needed**

By the seaside

What's so good about it?

• A dramatic rocky headland full of wild flowers • Sea birds and a view across to Wales • Rocky and pebbly coves • Grassy downland

Ⓐ Activities to enjoy:

• *Fly a kite (but only where it is safe)*
• *Make a beach mini shelter*
• *Search for fossils and interesting drift wood and stones*

What to take:

✔Kite; ✔rucksack; ✔light waterproof jacket; ✔good stout shoes or boots – wellington boots could be good for the beaches; ✔a small towel; ✔picnic or snacks; ✔water; ✔notebook and pen; ✔a camera.

START:

At the north end of Sand Bay. Sand Bay is on the coast between Weston-super-Mare and Clevedon. It can be approached from Weston along the toll road or through Worle and Kewstoke.

OS map Explorer 153 Weston-super-Mare and Bleadon Hill, grid ref. 330 659. (See **Activity No. 1** on page 50 for how to find a grid reference on a map.)

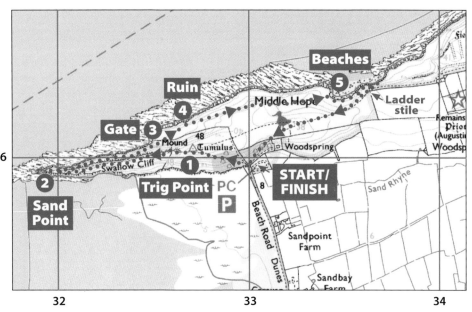

PARK:

In the National Trust car park at the North end of Sand Bay. If you want to know about the area look at the Information Board.

SETTING OFF:

Turn right from the car park and go steeply up the flight of steps.

Come out on to the open downland and reach a concrete triangulation pillar.

1.Trig Point

This is a Trig Point. They were set up years ago when there was a big project to map England. Surveyors put their measuring instruments on the top. They could see two other Trig Points and this helped them to work out a measuring triangle. Trig is short for 'triangulation'. They are used no longer because mapping is done with the use of satellite.

The most exciting route now is to walk out to Sand Point, where you need to take care – turn left and keep going out on the headland staying in the middle or over to the left.

✔

SPOT CHECK

Can you find this *thingy*?

Or you can simply leave the point out and go straight on. (Drop down onto a path along the edge and turn right.)

Notice how many wildflowers cling to the edges. You can see across Sand Bay to the old pier of Birnbeck Island sticking out. You can also see across the Severn Estuary to Wales. The two islands you can see are Flat Holm and Steep Holm.

Did you know that the Bristol Channel has the second largest rise and fall of tide in the world – about 14.3m (47 ft). The St Lawrence River in Canada has the greatest.

2. Sand Point
Go to the very end.

 Stop for a minute. What can you hear? It could be a good place for a photo.

Then turn round. Drop down to a grassy path above the edge keeping the water on your left. Just follow the edge along. Stay over to the left and choose one of the paths going on. Take care and don't run about here. Depending on the season you are likely to see wildflowers such as **pink thrift**,

rock samphire and the white flowered **sea campion**.

3. Gate
Go through a gate and come onto the open grassland. You reach a wide open grassy area.

 This is a great place for flying a kite (Activity No. 12).

*If you keep an eye out you may see a **sparrow hawk** hunting along the ridge, and lots of rabbits darting in and out of the bushes. You may also spot **orchids** and **cowslips**.*

Over on the right is a wall built by French prisoners over 150 years ago. You can also see ridges on the hillside. These are made by cows and sheep as they move along the side of the hill grazing.

4. Ruin
If you keep close to the edge you will reach a ruined stone shelter tucked into the back of a narrow rocky cove.

This was a hut used by men who came to fish for shrimps and they cooked them in a huge pot on a fire in the hut before selling them around Weston. Can you see where the fireplace was?

To carry on you need to scramble up the grassy bank. Continue on and soon get to the beaches of Middle Hope.

4. Beaches
 It's a great place to make your own stone mini shelter using anything you can find on the beaches.

 Here you may also hunt for interesting

stones and fossils and driftwood. Fossil hunters have been coming to Middle Hope and its beaches for centuries. It is a Site of Special Scientific Interest because of its volcanic rocks.

The volcanic ash preserved the fossils. You can see different species of corals, brachiopods, crinoids stems, worms, algae and other very early life forms. Hammering to find fossils and collecting them is banned. Just look and maybe take a photograph if you are lucky to find some.

Be careful not to go out into the water or on the mud.

How far you go on this walk now is up to you.

When you reach a wall ahead with a high ladder you can turn back. Just turn right across to the other side and turn right along the wall until you get to a footpath which takes you left down to the car park.

Or carry on. If you do, once you have crossed the ladder stile, stay up on the bank and then drop down left onto the grassy edge again. There are other beaches along here.

When you want to go back, turn right across to a track on the other side and turn right along the track. Then go through an opening in the wall ahead of you and carry on, following the wall on your left until you come to the footpath which goes down left to the car park.

Old tracks and tunnel

What's so good about it?

• A walk along the old Strawberry Line • A Time Line
• Old railway station • A natural spring • A railway tunnel

Ⓐ Activities to enjoy:

• *Identifying trees (in Summer)*
• *Work out the Time Line*
• *Have a picnic at the old station* • *Make a compass in a puddle*

What to take:

✔Waterproof jacket; ✔stout shoes or boots; ✔rucksack; ✔water; ✔picnic; ✔paper clip for compass in puddle; ✔notebook and pen; ✔a camera; ✔book of trees.

START:

Just south of Winscombe. OS map Explorer 141 Cheddar Gorge & Mendip Hills West, grid ref. 421 560 (see page 50 for how to find a grid reference on a map).

PARK:

At the King's Wood National Trust car park. This is just off the A38 between Winscombe and Cross. If coming from the north, pass a garage and then turn right on Winscombe Hill. The parking area is shortly on the left.

SETTING OFF:

Cross the road and go through a metal barrier on the bridleway. A short way down, bear right and up steps into a meadow called Slader's Leigh. This is owned and managed by the Mendip Society and is important because of the wildflowers and insects.

About mid May you are likely to see **orchids** *and also look out for* **frogs** *in the pond at the bottom. Enjoy the many* **butterflies** *and* **dragonflies**, *as well as* **crickets** *and* **grasshoppers**.

✔ SPOT CHECK

Can you find this *thingy*?

1. Railway Line

In the bottom right corner turn right and go down onto the old Strawberry Line.

It takes its name from the famous Cheddar strawberries which were carried along this railway, along with dairy produce and stone from Mendip quarries for nearly a century, until 1965. Now it is a cycle and walking route and a local nature reserve.

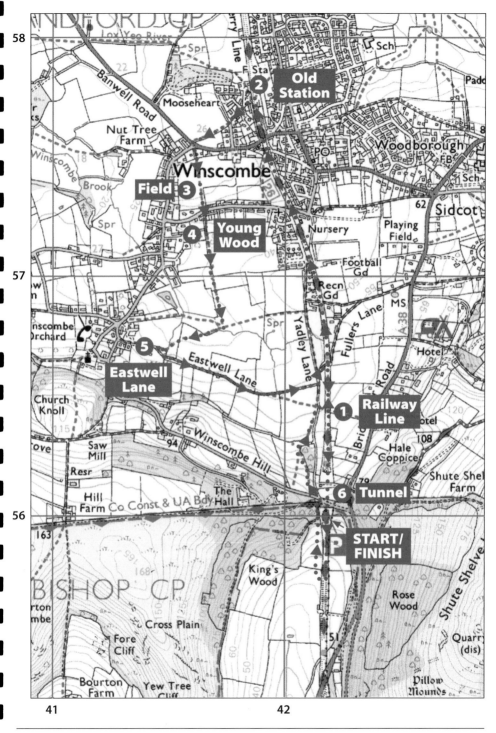

Old Station 2

Winscombe

Field 3

4 **Young Wood**

5 **Eastwell Lane**

1 **Railway Line**

6 **Tunnel**

START/ FINISH

Turn left.

A *There are a variety of trees along the line – three of our most common trees. On this page are some close up pictures of the leaves. Can you identify them? Answers on page 56.*

A: ....

B: ....

C: ....

Go through two sets of gates and continue on. Go under a railway bridge. Then the track crosses the road in Winscombe and reaches Old Station Green.

2. Old Station

Right at the start, by the wooden kissing gate on the right is a fascinating Time Line made up of paving slabs along the edge of the old platform. It traces our history from the Birth of Christ to the start of this Century and has metal plaques showing different events in history.

Q :**How many years does each slab represent?**

A *Read the information board so you can work out the lay-out of the old station. Stand in the old ticket office, etc. Imagine you are waiting for a train in about 1908. What clothes did you wear? How much was the ticket?*

A *Have a picnic.*

Go on to see the Millennium Green Sculpture.

*It looks like a pair of railway lines snaking into the distance. Some say that the '**SS**' stands for '**Strawberry Special**', the name given to the regular passenger service along the line.*

Alongside the sculpture, go left down a path with a wooden rail. Go through a gate at the foot and straight ahead on a stony path (don't turn left). Keep straight on along the road and at a bend, go on through a gate into a field.

3. Field

Follow the left hedge. Come out at the end on to a fairly busy road so take care. Cross and on the far side go over a stone slab stile and along a path. Come into a field and go straight across. On the far side by an electricity transformer go onto a path and follow it along to a road.

Turn left and immediately right on a tarmac path, Spring Walk, between houses. Stay close to the fence on the right and continue ahead on a path.

4. Young Wood
At the end go straight on into an emerging woodland. About two thirds of the way along, go right over a stone slab stile, just past a large horse chestnut tree.

Q: Why is it called a horse chestnut?

Carry on in the same direction. On the far side, go through a wooden wicket gate and across the next field to the far right corner. Turn right into the field at the side crossing a small stream.

Bear left now across the field and over a stile. Turn right and go across to a wide gap on the right. Go through into the next field and head diagonally up and across towards the far top corner.

Go right over a stile and across a stream, which has just risen a short way away up at the East Well. Cross. If you want to see this spring which for centuries was the source of water for Winscombe, turn up left by the stream for a few yards. To continue the walk, come back and carry on through the wood and reach Eastwell Lane.

5. Eastwell Lane
Turn left and follow it between hedges. It may be muddy in parts.

 Try making a compass in one of the puddles (Activity No. 7).

At the end come to another track – Yadley Lane. Turn left a short distance and then go right to take you back to the Strawberry Line again.

Turn right. Continue along here. Pass the gate where you came down earlier.

6. Tunnel
This huge tunnel was blasted out of solid rock in 1868.

 *How long do you think it is? Use your pacing to find out – Activity No. 10. (Answer on page 56.)*

Shortly after you enter the tunnel the solar lights along the ground in the centre should come on because of the sensors at each entrance.

7. Path
Leave the tunnel and shortly go right up a clear path. This climbs back up. Cross a stile and immediately turn steeply up right through King's Wood and come up to a cottage and gate on the right into the car park.

Worth the efFORT!

What's so good about it?

• A mixture of forest and open walking • An Iron Age hillfort

A **Activities to enjoy:**

- *Build a mini shelter from sticks*
- *Fly a kite*
- *Track*
- *Make a compass in a puddle*

What to take:

✔Rucksack; ✔waterproof jacket; ✔good stout shoes or boots; ✔picnic or snack; ✔water; ✔kite; ✔notebook and pen; ✔a camera; ✔a paper clip and magnet (for the compass).

START:
At Rowberrow hamlet. From the Churchill traffic lights, go south on the A38. Go uphill and then left to Rowberrow. OS Explorer map 141, Cheddar Gorge & Mendip Hills West, grid ref. 450 582 (see page 50 for how to find a map grid reference).

PARK:
At the spacious Swan Inn car park, opposite the pub. Please check that it is OK to park here.

SETTING OFF:
Go down School Lane at the side of the pub and along through the hamlet, passing the old school. Continue on and drop quite steeply downhill.

1. Cottage
The track you reach at the bottom was the Slaggers Path – a route taken by miners from Shipham and Rowberrow in the c19th looking for work at the minelries at Charterhouse.

Reach a whitewashed cottage with shutters. Turn left alongside it and enter Rowberrow

Warren. Go uphill on the track into Rowberrow Forest.

2. Junction
Reach a junction at the top and bear left on the track, going along with a field on your right. The track begins to drop down.

A *Start to collect sticks to make a mini shelter (Activity No. 6).*

Ignore the first turn left, and take the second, continuing in the forest climbing some of the time on a good broad track. It bears left, (as a grassy track continues ahead), and takes you downhill.

3. Stony track
At the bottom, go left a yard or so to a T-junction with a stony track and turn right. It rises and brings you up to another T-junction. Turn left.

4. Dolbury Warren
After about 80 metres find a sign for Dolbury Warren on the left and cross the stile. This is National Trust land and is

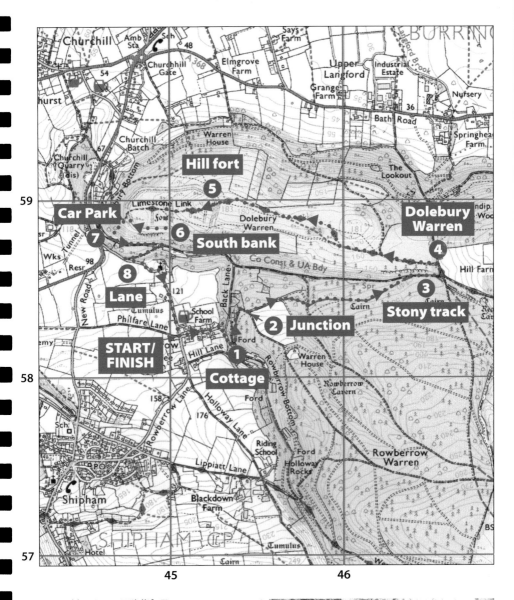

Map labels:

Churchill · Amb Sta · Sch · 48 · Churchhill Gate · Elmgrove Farm · Says Farm · Upper Langford · Industrial Estate · BURRINGTON · Langford Brook · Grange Farm · Nursery · 54 · hurst · 36 · Bath Road · Springhead Farm · Churchill Batch · Warren House · The Lookout · Churchill Quarry (dis) · 67

Hill fort
5

59 · Limestone Link · **Car Park** · Dolebury Warren · **Dolebury Warren** · ndip Woo · **7** · **6** · **South bank** · **4** · Hill Farm · Wks · Tunnel · Resr · 98 · Co Const & UA Bdy · 160 · **3** · **Stony track** · **8** · **Lane** · 121 · New Road · Back Lane · Spr · Cairn · Tumulus · Philfare Lane · School Farm · **2** · **Junction** · **1** · **Cottage** · Ford · Warren House · Rowberrow Cavern

START/ FINISH · Hill Lane

58 · 158 · Rowberrow Lane · Holloway Lane · Ford · Rowberrow Bottom · Rowberrow Warren · Sch · 176 · Riding School · Ford · Holloway Rocks · Lippiatt Lane · Shipham · Blackdown Farm · Hotel · SHIPHAM CP · Cairn · Tumulus · 249

57

45 · 46

managed by Avon Wildlife Trust.

Now comes the open land – a good stretch straight ahead up the close cropped grassland. This area often has a good selection of wildflowers.

Cross a stile by a wooden gate and carry on, climbing .

Saxons. There is no evidence that it was ever attacked. This is one of the most beautiful viewpoints on Mendip.

You can let your imagination free as you sit up here and soak up the view. Years ago you may have watched Roman war galleys putting in at the mouth of the Axe; may have watched the sea-fight that drove the pirates of Brittany over to Wales.

(A) *This could be a good place to try out your kite, or wait until you get higher.*

Go over another stile by a gate and keep going. Near woodland, find a post with a yellow Limestone Link marker and turn right.

The Limestone Link is about 58km long and links two limestone areas – the Cotswolds and Mendip.

At the next marker post, turn left and go through woodland.

(A) *Anywhere up here would be a good place for tracking (Activity No. 9).*

(A) *This is also a good place for making a mini shelter (Activity No. 6).*

Continue on, out into the open and on up. Go over another stile by a gate.

Reach the outer bank and opening of Dolbury hillfort. This side is on the East and was the weakest so it has a double bank to defend it.

Go through onto this Iron Age Hill fort.

5. Hill Fort
Dolebury was later used by the Romans and

Go straight ahead and come to a bumpy stony mound, the remains of a warrener's house.

A warrener's job was to look after the rabbit warren to provide food for the local people. More than 20 traps were set up and there were also long 'pillow mounds' to encourage the rabbits to burrow and breed within the hill fort.

Continue straight on down the centre and reach another track coming in from the left. Join this, more or less continuing in the same direction. About now it is a good idea to go left across the rough grass to the southern bank of the hillfort.

6. South Bank
*See how steep the side is. It would have been difficult to attack the fort from here. This grassy warm southern slope is a favourite basking spots for **adders**.*

WARNING! Don't try flying your kite here close to this steep edge!

Turn right along the bank – either the upper one, or the lower one – keeping the steep slope on your left. In the south west corner, look for a small path and then steps. Follow these steeply down.

7. Car Park

At the foot, cross a stile into a parking area.

(A) *It is often wet here so it would be good for making a compass in a puddle (Activity No. 7).*

Turn left through a gate and follow the track. After about 350 metres, turn right onto a footpath (by a gate marked 'private'). This stony path climbs up to the road.

8. Road

Turn left and after a few minutes reach Rowberrow church.

Continue on round the bend and up the road to the Swan, a very well known family pub and popular with walkers.

✔ SPOT CHECK

Can you find this *thingy*?

The Swan, Rowberrow, open daily, tel: 01934 852371.

Ponies and a dew pond

What's so good about it?

• A beautiful area of open land and woods with Exmoor ponies and a dewpond

Ⓐ Activities to enjoy:

• *Fly a kite* • *Track*
• *Make a mini shelter*
• *Make and sail your own boat*
• *Take a picnic to eat on Long Rock*

What to take:

✔Your kite; ✔rucksack; ✔a waterproof jacket;
✔good stout shoes or boots; ✔notebook and pen; ✔a camera; ✔bring a book of trees if you have one.

START:

At Burrington Ham which is at the top of Burrington Combe. OS map Explorer 141 Cheddar Gorge & Mendip Hills West, grid ref. 489 581 (see page 50 for how to find a grid reference).

PARK:

Burrington Ham has a the parking lay-by on the left near the top. There is often an ice cream van. This road is the B3134 across Mendip from the A368 Churchill to Blagdon road. When parking do not block the stony track onto the Ham.

SETTING OFF:

Go up the wide rocky track leading out the back of the parking area on the left. Come up on to Burrington Ham.

Ⓐ *This open area is a great place to fly your kite. Either do it now or when you return (Activity No. 12).*

1. Marker Post

Reach a marker post.

Q: **What do a yellow and blue arrow show? (Answers on page 56.)**

Turn left and you are now walking on a ridge of land. Across on your left is Black Down, the highest point of Mendip (325m) and over right is Wrington Vale and views across the Severn Estuary.

*Anywhere up on the Ham, either on the open land or in the woods, you may see a group of **Exmoor ponies**. They were brought here to graze the land, to keep it open and to encourage wild flowers. In Spring you can see a great display of **bluebells** here. The ponies*

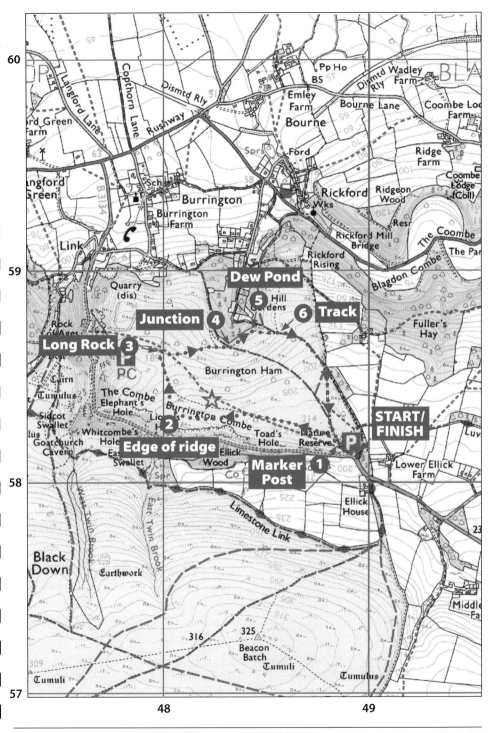

Dew Pond

5

Hill dens

6 Track

Junction **4**

Long Rock **3**

Burrington Ham

2

Edge of ridge

Marker Post **1**

START/ FINISH

are doing a good job. They are not pets, so don't try to pat or feed them and keep your dog under control.

In Spring and Summer keep your eyes open for flowers such as **wild thyme** on the anthills, **wild marjoram**, **salad burnett** and **rock rose**.

After about five minutes you can take one of the main paths which fork left. Come to an open area above Burrington Combe. Be careful because there is a steep edge here and control your dog.

2. End of ridge
Carry on to the end of the open area on the ridge. Then turn down right downhill. Can you see rocks up ahead? We are going there.

✔ SPOT CHECK

Can you find these waymarks?

Above you may well see a **kestrel** hovering, a **buzzard** soaring on the warm air rising from the combe. Sometimes you may see **ravens** tumbling out of the sky or hear their 'kronking' call.

3. Long Rock
Reach Long Rock and climb up to enjoy the views and maybe have a snack.

You should be able to see Blagdon Lake down on the right. Also you may well be able to see planes arriving and leaving Bristol airport. Can you see the two bridges across the Severn Estuary?

As you come off the rocks, bear left on the wide grassy track. (If you didn't go up on the rocks, just bear right on the track). This drops downhill into the wooded valley.

A *This is a good place to make a mini shelter using dry sticks (Activity No. 6).*

A *Any time now you can start to do some tracking. You can go off the path here as it is Open Access but you need to take care. Also start to collect sticks to make a boat.*

4. Junction
Reach a T-junction with another track. Go straight across. This is a smaller path which the ponies have made.

5. Dew Pond

Lined with stone and clay, this collects rainwater and water running off the land – not much dew!

There is a great shortage of natural ponds on Mendip which is made of limestone and so doesn't hold water. Instead, the water drains underground and forms streams. There are great caverns and pot holes under Mendip where people enjoy caving. The water under Mendip provides drinking water for Bristol thanks to the work of Bristol Water which was set up in 1846.

A **Why not make a small boat from sticks and sail it on the pond. Put it into the undergrowth when you have finished so it can rot away naturally.**

From the dew pond carry on along a path continuing in the same direction as before. You go through bracken and trees. Reach another crossing track.

6. Track

Turn right, climbing uphill and this brings you back to the open Ham.

A **You may like to try your kite here again, or for the first time.**

Go back down to the car parking area.

Lake and hill

What's so good about it?

• Walk close beside a lake • Climb one hill and get your heart working well • Follow a stream • Visit a wildflower meadow by the lake

Activities to enjoy:

- *Make a grass whistle*
- *Bird watch*
- *Estimate the age of an oak*
- *Race sticks on a stream*
- *Picnic in a wildflower meadow*

What to take:

✔Rucksack; ✔waterproof jacket; ✔good stout shoes or boots; ✔picnic or snacks; ✔water; ✔binoculars and maybe a bird book, if you can, for bird watching; ✔notebook and pen; ✔a camera.

START:

At Blagdon Lake which is just north of Blagdon village. OS Explorer map 141 Cheddar Gorge & Mendip Hills West, grid ref. 504 603 (see page 50 for how to work out a grid reference).

PARK:

On the north side of the dam along the road which runs from Blagdon to Butcombe. Park by the metal kissing gate.

SETTING OFF:

This reservoir and the 640 metre dam was a huge project by Bristol Water at the end of the c19th. It took eight years for the work to be done by labourers with horse-drawn carts. Materials were brought to the site along a branch railway. The lake holds about 7,720 million litres of water. Learn more at Bristol Water's visitor centre at the other end of the dam (details at the end).

Go through the kissing gate and immediately follow the lake edge. This is a very popular trout fishing lake.

A *There are some individual oak trees along here. Can you choose one and work out its age? (Activity No. 2).*

1. Footbridge

Reach a plank bridge and cross it.

Q: **Guess how many planks there are (answer on page 56).**

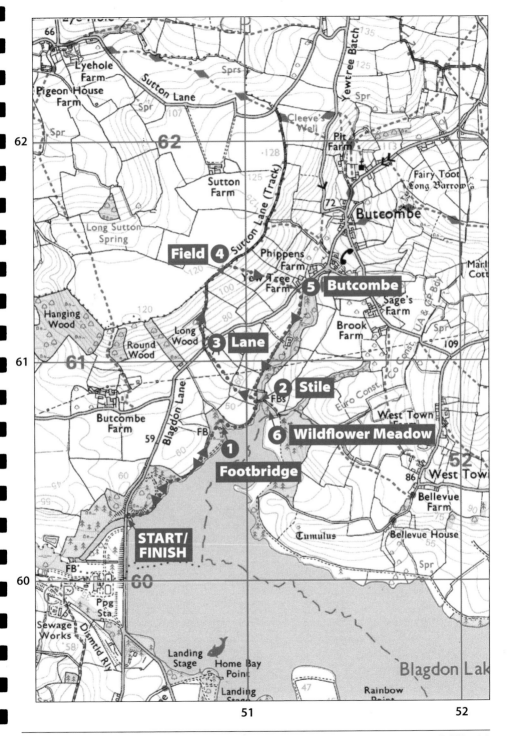

START/FINISH

1 Footbridge

2 Stile

3 Lane

4 Field

5 Butcombe

6 Wildflower Meadow

Carry on.

A *There should be some good grasses along here for trying your hand at a grass whistle (Activity No. 8).*

2. Stile
Just before the next footbridge, turn left and cross a stile into a field. Go up to the top right corner.

A *This could be a good field for trying to find your own lucky four-leaf clover.*

*It's very rare to find a four-leaf clover (the chances are 1 in 10,000 three-leaved clovers). According to tradition, it brings good luck. Each leaf represents something: the first is for **hope**, the second is for **faith**, the third is for **love**, and the fourth is for **luck**.*

Clovers can have more than four leaves: the most ever recorded is 21 – a Guinness World Record set in June 2008.

Go through into another field. Now follow the left hedge up to a large metal gate onto a lane.

3. Lane
Cross and go up the track opposite by a house. This is the start of a 7 minute climb up the hill. The track is an old route called Sutton Lane.

The track becomes rougher, and sunken but then levels out and you are on the top. Reach two stately beech trees on the right. Cross the stile at the side of the beeches. It has a footpath arrow.

4. Field
You are now at the top of a field with a great view over Blagdon Lake. You are looking across the Yeo Valley which lends its name to the famous company that sells its yogurt and dairy products in this country and around the world. The farm where this great business started is situated on the other side of the lake.

Go down the grassy hill – either walking or maybe a run! Cross a stile in the fence below – about a third of the way along from the bottom left corner. Go under a line of trees and over another stile. Now head down to the bottom left corner, just to the right of the farmhouse. Cross over onto a path, which may be rather overgrown. Take care at the bottom – it is uneven and brings you straight onto the road. Keep your dog under control.

5. Butcombe
Turn left on the road and after about a minute go right through an unmarked opening into woods, crossing a stream. Bear right following the stream. Reach a wide concrete bridge over the stream with a large pool on one side.

A *This is a good place for stick racing. You need to place your sticks carefully to avoid them getting caught on the rocks (Activity No. 5)!*

Continue through the woodland and come to a gate and stile on the right. Cross and go up the track a metre or two and then go left over a stile. Keep the woodland on your left through this field and through the next. Then reach the stile you were at earlier. Cross left.

6. Wildflower meadow
Detour: This Is only a few minutes and a great place to go, especially for a picnic: Go straight on over the large plank bridge. Then cross right over a barrier stile on the far side and follow a path through the woods. Cross over onto a path and go over

another bridge. Go along the path a few metres and turn right into a beautiful open area – a sunny wildflower meadow going right down to the lake edge and looking across to the Mendip Hills and Blagdon.

Retrack your steps back along the lake edge to where you started.

Visitor Centre

On the other end of the dam is Bristol Water's Pumping Station and Visitor Centre.
The Gothic style building was put up to house four massive steam driven beam engines. Together these meant that about 34 million litres of water could be pumped each day.

Two of the beam engines were preserved as museum pieces. The boiler house is now a great visitor centre with demonstrations and exhibitions. Displays show the wildlife and nature conservation around the lake. There are also rooms about water conservation techniques in the home and garden and a special area to show the work of Water Aid in India and Africa.

Blagdon Beam Engine and Visitor centre is usually open on Sunday afternoons from the beginning of May to the

✔ SPOT CHECK

Can you find this *thingy*?

end of August. Entry and parking is free.

Go to the Blagdon Centre section on the Bristol Water website to find out more.

For more details call 0117 953 6470 or visit
www.bristolwater.co.uk/leisure

The Grebe and Bittern trail

What's so good about it?

• A nature trail beside Chew Valley Lake with an amazing bird hide

Ⓐ Activities to enjoy:

• *Watch out for a wide variety of birds at all times of year*
• *Make a leaf rubbing*
• *Guess the height and age of an oak tree*
• *Find a pine cone – and take it home as a natural barometer*
• *Make a mini shelter*
• *Look for animal tracks*
• *Make a grass whistle*

What to take:

✔*Binoculars and maybe a bird book and book of trees;* ✔*rucksack;* ✔*waterproof jacket;* ✔*good stout shoes or boots;* ✔*notebook and pen;* ✔*a camera.*

Dogs are welcome but must be kept on a lead to avoid disturbing wildlife.

START:

On the north shore of Chew Valley Lake. OS map Explorer 155 Bristol & Bath, grid ref. 577 607 (see page 50 for how to find a grid reference on a map.)

PARK :

There are two public parking areas along the north side of the lake on the road from Chew Stoke to Bishop Sutton. You want No. 2. From Chew Stoke go past the larger one which has a café and keep on for about half a mile to the second. Go down to the parking area and turn left. There may be a charge for parking.

Our circle is a combination of the **Grebe** *and* **Bittern Trails** *devised by Bristol Water. You can buy the two leaflets at the café in the first car park.*

Remember: Keep as quiet as possible and keep your eyes and ears open to spot animals and birds. The slower you go and the more time you take, the more wildlife you will see.

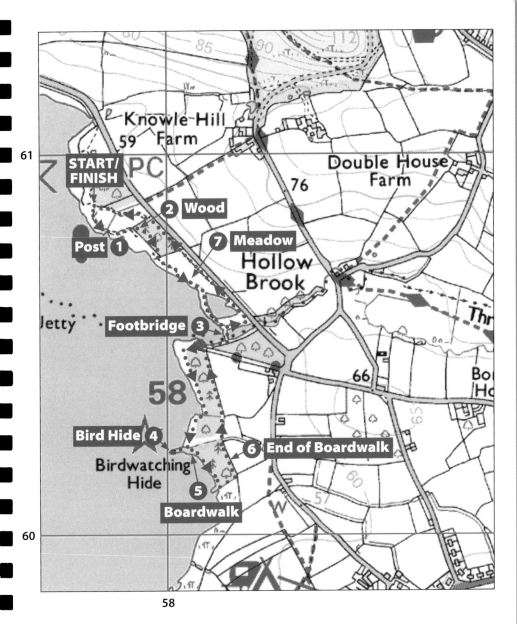

SETTING OFF:

Chew Valley Lake open in 1956 by the Queen provides vital drinking water for the area. It is owned and managed by Bristol Water. The company has set up this wonderful recreational area alongside the lake for the public.

Facing the lake go to the far left end, walk out by a semi circular seating area and fork right on the Grebe Trail which has numbered information posts on the way.

This trail is hard surfaced.

1.Post

Opposite **Post 1** is an alder tree, an important wetland tree (see image above).

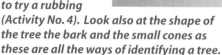

Alder

Ⓐ **Why not take a leaf home** to try a rubbing (Activity No. 4). Look also at the shape of the tree the bark and the small cones as these are all the ways of identifying a tree.

Go through the reed beds which are a much used habitat for wildlife.

Ⓐ *In the reedbeds look out for **reed buntings** with brown plumage – a smarter version of the **house sparrow**.*

2. Wood

Bend left into woodland. This has sweet chestnut, beech, sycamore, oak, hornbeam, larch and corsican pine. Here, too, are scots pine.

Ⓐ *Find a pine cone (depending on the season) to take home as a natural barometer. In dry weather, pine cones open out as the scales shrivel up and stand out stiffly. When it is damp, they absorb moisture and as the scales become flexible again, the cone returns to its normal shape.*

Ⓐ *Lookout for birds in the woodland too – such as **coal tits** up in the pines, **chaffinches** or maybe the small, brown **tree creeper** as it looks for insects in the bark.*

Come out of the wood and rejoin the path and reach **Post 3** and carry on.

Many birds search the reed beds for food such as insects and use the beds for breeding and for security.

Ⓐ *Look for large flocks of **tits**, (**blue, great, coal** and **long-tailed**) and the tiny **goldcrest**. In summer you may hear the song of the **reed warblers** (jag-jag-jag-kerr-kerr-kerr) and **sedge warblers** (a sharp tuc-tuc-tuc).*

The winding path takes you through an open area. Pass **Post 4** and soon, on the left just by a pond, reach an oak tree.

Ⓐ *Try guessing its height and age (Activities No. 2 and 3). It's a good open flat area to try this out.*

Continue to follow the trail past **Post 5**. Carry on, going through more woodland and eventually passing boulders and reach a path junction where the Bittern Trail branches off .

3. Footbridge

Cross the wooden footbridge and follow the Bittern Trail right. This trail doesn't have numbered posts

Ⓐ *Look out for badger footprints in the damp earth.*

Stay on the Trail for several minutes until you reach a long wooden boardwalk. Don't start along it yet, but instead turn right and go along a path past screening and reach the bird hide. Note the wonderful old fallen willow tree on the right just before the hide – a great habitat for insects.

4. Bird Hide

Ⓐ *This is a wonderful quiet place named after an exceptional birdwatcher, Bernard King, overlooking Spring Bay where you can watch many different birds – **canada geese, coots** and **heron** – at any time of year. In winter the lake attracts numbers of less common duck such as **gadwall, shoveller, teal** and **pochard**.*

In March **swallows** and **martins** arrive and during the summer swoop overhead and skim over the reedbeds and open water, leaving again in October or November. **Swifts** arrive a bit later and stay only for about three months.

You may see a **cormorant** in late summer, sitting on a post with its wings out to dry. There are sure to be many species of duck, and the bay is a good feeding area for waders on their autumn passage – **lapwing, sandpiper, greenshanks, snipe** and **dunlin**. Out in the open water you may see **great crested grebes** fishing. In spring and summer you could be lucky and see them carrying their young on their backs.

The hide also overlooks Denny Island a safe nesting sige for birds like the **great crested grebe, mallard, tufted duck** and especially **canada geese**.

Go back to the start of the boardwalk.

5. Boardwalk

Go along this great dry route nearly to the end and reach a left hand bend.

(If you want to cut the walk short, continue on the boardwalk and at the end turn left and pick up the trail from '6. End of Boardwalk'.)

But to enjoy the full **Bittern Trail**, leave the boardwalk at the bend and go straight on down two steps and along the grassy path. It eventually bends round left and on past woodland.

 Further along here could be a good place to stop and make a mini shelter

using some of the dead sticks on the ground (Activity No. 6).

Pass the far end of the boardwalk.

6. End of Boardwalk

Just continue on your path with open fields now on the right. Reach the point where the **Grebe** and **Bittern Trails** meet where you were earlier. Turn right back through the open area and past the boulders and go left back over the footbridge and turn right back on the **Grebe Trail** and follow the edge round an open area.

 This could be a good place for making a grass whistle (Activity No. 8).

7. Meadow

Past **Post 7** which tells you about the butterflies and wildflowers you may see here.

Retrace your steps to the car park.

✓ **SPOT CHECK**

Shoveller

Where can you find this drawing of a *shoveller duck*?

The ancient stones

What's so good about it?

- Beautiful Somerset countryside
- An amazing viaduct
- The ancient standing stones
- The River Chew

Ⓐ Activities to enjoy:

- *Ley line hunting* • *Race sticks*
- *Make a grass whistle* • *Hunt a four leaf clover*
- *Imagine the history of the great stones and the rituals that took place there*
- *Look on website to see what the standing stones used to look like*

What to take:

✔*Your homemade dowsing rods made from metal coat hangers (Activities p.55);* ✔*rucksack;*
✔*a waterproof jacket;* ✔*good stout shoes or boots;* ✔*notebook and pen;* ✔*a camera.*

START:

At Pensford, a few miles south of Bristol on the A37. OS Explorer Map 153, Bristol & Bath, grid ref. 620 638

PARK:

At the village hall car park which is well signed – if coming from Bristol, cross the bridge and turn left and left again up Publow Lane. The hall is along on the left.

SETTING OFF:

Turn right towards the village and at the junction pass the old dome-roofed c18th village lock-up *(left)* which is now a Scheduled Ancient Monument.

Continue to the main road and turn right over the bridge.

Just as well you weren't here in 1968. There was a terrible storm and the River Chew flooded. The bridge was swept away.

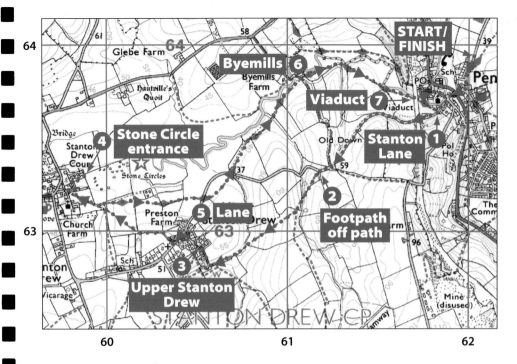

Take the pedestrian crossing to the other side and then go along towards the village store and turn left down by the Rising Sun pub. Pass the church. Cross the river again on an older bridge by a grand old mill.

This was one of many woollen mills along the River Chew.

1.Stanton Lane

Turn right up Stanton Lane and shortly go under the magnificent viaduct built in 1873 to carry the Bristol and North Somerset Railway over the River Chew. The big flood of 1968 damaged this mighty viaduct which never reopened.

Look up and imagine the men who laboured long and hard to produce this

Q: **How many arches are there? (Answer on page 56.)**

Continue along the quiet lane. Along the edge are several old ash trees that have had the tops cut off – pollarded.

Pass a footpath signpost and carry on a bit further.

✔ SPOT CHECK

Can you find this arch?

2. Footpath
Very shortly, down in the dip, go left through a metal kissing gate following the footpath.

A kissing gate is so called because the gate, as it swings, just lightly touches the frame – or 'kisses' it.

Go diagonally across the field, and over a footbridge and continue across the next field. After another metal gate, go up into a field and go round the right edge, soon getting some good views across the countryside towards Stanton Drew.

(A) ***There may be some good grasses here to try making a grass whistle (Activity No. 8).***

In the far left corner go through a gate and over a bridge. Continue with the stream and field edge on your left and in the corner a gate brings you to the end of a drive. Turn right past houses and continue on and round a bend to the main village road.

3. Upper Stanton Drew
Cross the road and turn left up the raised pavement.

Shortly, turn right up a footpath between cottages. Go through one gate and on to another. Here you come into a field. Can you see some of the standing stones in a field ahead in the distance?

Go diagonally down the centre of the field. Just short of the bottom corner, go left through a metal kissing gate marked with a footpath arrow. Turn right and come onto a concrete farm drive (you may need to duck under an electric wire).

Go up this drive and reach a crossing path which links two of the stone circles. This is not the entrance to the main stones. Continue up the track to the end. Turn sharp right and follow this road along and left.

4. Stone Circles
Turn right to the gate and entrance to the Circles, cared for by English Heritage. £1 entrance. Your dog will have to wait here.

Two of the three Stone Circles are in this field. The largest being the Great Circle – one of the largest in the country – and the other, the North East Circle.

About ten years ago a special survey of the site made an amazing discovery. Beneath the stones and around them is a pattern of wooden posts. It was thought to be the largest structure in the country with pits, ditches and fireplaces.

Stanton Drew was a place of great significance during the later Stone Age.

(A) ***Try your hand at ley line hunting (See Activity No. 13, page 55). Walk slowly and see if your dowsing rods find any energies. It can be great fun.***

You can either go back out the way you came in and then return down the farm track to the crossing point. Or turn right and go across the Stone Circle field to the stile onto the farm track.

Go back down the concrete track, retracing your steps of earlier and go through the metal kissing gate into the field.

Now go straight on with the hedge on the left.

(A) *This may be a good place to look for a four leaf clover (see Blagdon walk on page 18).*

Go through a gate in the hedge ahead. You want to keep in this direction, but to do this you need to go left and right. Carry on then and go through another field.

5. Lane
Come to a lane.

Cross and take the footpath opposite. Go through a large metal gate. Follow the left edge of the field to a metal gate on the left. This brings you back onto the lane.

Go straight over into a field and follow the left hedge along. Go left through a metal gate and now head on towards the River Chew, following it along on the left through fields. On the way go through a gate. Eventually a wooden kissing gate brings you to Byemills.

6. Byemills
Go left a short way to the bridge over the Chew.

(A) *This is a great place for stick racing (Activity No. 5).*

To continue, go straight on up the wide grassy path by the house. Come into a meadow and keep straight on. Go through a gate and on. Ahead is the viaduct again.

7. Viaduct
Go under it. Bear left over the river and follow the path to the garden of the Rising Sun pub by an old weir.

From the pub, go through the parking area opposite and up steps onto the road bridge. Turn right and retrace your steps back to where you parked.

The Rising Sun, Pensford, 01761 490402

The Druids Arms, Stanton Drew, 01275 332230, closed Mondays

Useful websites:
http://www.digitaldigging.co.uk/models/ stanton/reconstructions_stanton_drew_ info_page.html
http://www.isleofavalon.co.uk/ sacredsites/stantondrew.html

Following Jack and Jill

What's so good about it?

• Cycle/scooter an old railway line and then climb up Jack and Jill Hill

Ⓐ Activities to enjoy:

• *Riding along and following in the footsteps of Jack and Jill*
• *Have a homemade snack somewhere along the route up the hill or on the bench seats along the railway line.*
• *Build a mini shelter*

What to take:

✔ *A waterproof;* ✔ *rucksack;* ✔ *homemade snack;* ✔ *notebook and pencil;* ✔ *a camera.*

NB: This is a cycle and walk!

Make your way by bike or scooter along the disused rail line, the Colliers Way, for half the walk, and then it's walking in the steps of Jack and Jill up the hill in Kilmersdon. There is a good café either at the start or the end. (Of course, you can walk the whole way, there and back, if you wish.)

START:

In Radstock. OS Explorer map 142, Shepton Mallet and Mendip Hills East, grid ref. 688 547

PARK:

At the free car park in Station Road, Radstock. To find it, go to the junction by the Co-op in the centre of Radstock, and cross into Fortescue Road. Pass shops and go straight on at the junction. Continue for a few more metres and turn up right to the car park.

SETTING OFF:

Unload your cycles/scooters and turn right from the car park and go past the church. Continue along the road, cross the river, and soon turn left in Meadow View. This turns into a track at the end. Follow it on and over

a bridge and up to join the old railway line, now the Colliers Way. It is named after the local coalminers.

1. Colliers Way

Turn right along the route where as you can see the old line is still there. Imagine the journeys that must have been taken along here in the past.

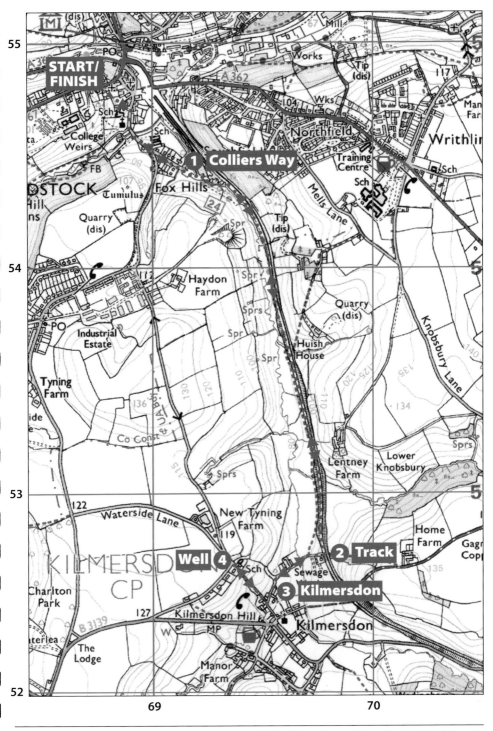

START/FINISH

1 Colliers Way

2 Track

3 Kilmersdon

Well **4**

You are in good company on your bikes as the Colliers Way is part of the National Cycle Network that is set to run from Dundas near Bath to Southampton! This is the route of the old North Somerset Railway between Radstock and Frome which ran from 1854 through to the 1980s.

Pass a Colliers Way board which sets the scene for our walk. Take time to read it.

After a while the going becomes more open and you can see across the rolling Somerset farmland. Soon see Kilmersdon church and village ahead on the right.

2. Path
As you near the village, pass a flight of

steps down on the right and then reach a track which turns sharp right down off the Colliers Way. Bend round left and in the rough grass on the left notice a large stone boulder. This gives the names of the apple trees planted nearby and along the Collier's Way.

Artists worked on this project with local schools to develop a' Linear Orchard' along the old track, consisting of English apples trees to highlight the disappearing orchards in Somerset and echo self-seeded fruit trees (from apples cores thrown by train passengers).

3. Kilmersdon
Continue towards the village. As you draw closer to the centre pass an old charity school on the left, circa 1703.

Come to the foot of Jack and Jill Hill – the first turning on the right.

This was named after a local couple who used to go regularly up the steep hill to the well, and whose tumble gave rise to the popular nursery

rhyme. It is of course difficult to separate fact from fiction!

On the way up pass stones, giving the individual lines of the rhyme

4. Well

Reach the well at the top, by the primary school.

The Jack and Jill Millennium project discovered a Medieval well shaft in 1999, and built this well head over the 38ft deep well. Also notice the children's slate drawings on the wall of the school.

Turn round and go downhill and get back on your bikes and retrace your steps up to the railway line and back. In Radstock, don't forget to stop for a well deserved drink and snack at the Free Trade Centre and café on the left just before the church.

SPOT CHECK

Can you find this plaque?

Little Jack Horner's village

What's so good about it?

• Walk through and around Little Jack Horner's village

🅐 Activities to enjoy:

• *Practise your pacing*
• *Build a mini shelter*
• *Estimate the height and age of a tree*
• *Picnic by a stream*
• *Make and sail your own boat or raft*

What to take:

✔Rucksack; ✔waterproof jacket; ✔good stout shoes or boots; ✔a small towel; ✔picnic or snacks; ✔water; ✔notebook and pen; ✔biodegradable garden string; ✔a camera.

START:

Mells village. This is in East Mendip, just South West of Frome. OS map Explorer 142 Shepton Mallet & Mendip Hills East, grid ref: 730 490 (see page 50 for how to find a grid reference on a map).

PARK:

On the verge opposite the village shop at a junction of roads and a grassy area by the stream.

SETTING OFF:

Cross the road to the shop.

🅐 *Why not stop at the end for an ice cream? It is a community shop run by volunteers.*

Turn left and go up onto the raised path by a row of cottages. Drop back down to the road.

1.War Memorial

Pass the war memorial and shortly go on past a huge tithe barn over the road.

A tithe barn was used centuries ago for storing the tithes – a tenth of what a farmer grew. This was a tax to be paid to the church.

See ahead of you the Talbot Inn.

Q: Look up at the pub sign – what do you think a Talbot was? (Answer on page 56.)

Before you get there,

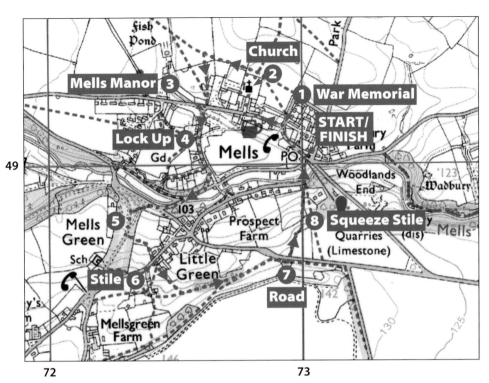

Map labels:
- Fish Pond
- Church **2**
- Park
- Mells Manor **3**
- **1** War Memorial
- START/FINISH
- Lock Up **4**
- Gd
- Mells PO
- Woodlands End
- Wadbury
- 49
- 103
- Mells Green **5**
- Prospect Farm
- **8** Squeeze Stile
- Quarries (dis)
- (Limestone)
- Mells
- Sch
- Stile **6**
- Little Green
- **7**
- Road
- Mellsgreen Farm

72

73

turn right up a short street which leads to the church.

This was called New Street but is over 525 years old. It was designed by the Abbot of Glastonbury to be the start of a village designed in the shape of a cross. But, this was the only street finished.

2.Church
Go into the churchyard.

The church is a very fine one with sculpture, monuments and art work by many famous artists who were friends of the Horner family in Mells Manor next door.

In the churchyard on the right hand side of the church is a grave to a famous war poet called **Siegfried Sassoon**. *It is a very simple grave. Can you find it?*

Go round the left side of the church and

you can see the Manor next door. Round the back go out down the fine avenue of yew trees.

Come into a field. Turn left and go over a stile. Go along with the wall of Mells Manor on your left.

Cross another stile ahead and carry on. A little way along the fence, climb left over a stile. Now go straight down with the manor on your left.

 Here is a good place to estimate the height and age of a tree. Choose one and have a go (Activities No. 2 and 3).

Go through a gate in the corner onto a lane. From here you can get a good view of the manor.

 Why not take a photo?

3. Mells Manor

The manor was the home of the Horner family for 400 years from the 16th century and it seems that the first Horner at Mells was Little Jack Horner himself!

He may have been the Steward to the Bishop of Glastonbury. All was well until Henry VIII (8th) tried to seize the Abbey. The Bishop wanting to save the Abbey thought he could bribe the King by giving him Mells Manor. It is said that the deed was hidden in a large pie to be taken by Horner to the King. On the way Horner opened up the pie and took the deeds to Mells manor for himself!

This is probably just a story. The nursery rhyme was published nearly 400 years ago in 1725.

Go straight over the road and up the lane past some pretty thatched cottages.

4. Lock Up

On the right is the lock-up, known also as a blind house, 1728, and opposite an arched stone grotto in the wall that used to contain a drinking trough.

Follow the lane down and round to a road.

Cross over and follow the footpath opposite uphill through trees. Come to an open green.

5. Green

Just before the village school, turn left across the grass following the footpath sign. Go over a stile and cross the field. Bend right to the corner where you cross over on to a lane.

6. Stile

Can you see the stile on the other side? Go over this and on the other side find the stony path up the bank through woodland.

A *Collect sticks so that you can make a boat or a raft for the end of the walk. Look out for a good leaf or feather for the sail.*

Come into a field and follow the left edge. Go by a telegraph post and keep on into another field. Just follow the left edge round. Then follow a line of telegraph poles across the field.

A *Measure the distance between the poles using your pacing (Activity No. 10). Answer on page 56.*

7. Road
Find the stile on the other side. Just before it, in the trees, you can see a warning notice about the quarry blasting. You may have heard the hooter.

Cross the road, which may be quite busy, and the stile on the other side. Cross the field to a hedge corner and turn right along the hedge.

8. Squeeze Stile
Near the end, go through a squeeze stile on your left.

Go down the right hedge to the bottom

✔ SPOT CHECK

Can you find this statue and who is it of?

corner. Go through another squeeze stile and down a short path to the lane. Keep straight on crossing the Mells Stream to where you started.

A *If you have time have a picnic or make your boat or raft and sail it here.*

Castle and stream

What's so good about it?
- A fantastic c14th castle • Wonderful wooden animal sculptures
- A stream to follow • Woods • Open land.

(A) Activities to enjoy:
- *Explore the castle*
- *Stick races on the stream*
- *Make and blow your own grass whistle*
- *Have a picnic by the stream or castle*
- *Look for faces and shapes in the trees*

What to take:
✔Rucksack; ✔light waterproof jacket; ✔good stout shoes or boots; ✔a small towel; ✔picnic or snacks; ✔water; ✔notebook and pen; ✔a camera.

START:
Nunney village. This is in East Mendip, just South West of Frome. OS map Explorer 142 Shepton Mallet & Mendip Hills East, grid ref: 734 456 (see page 50 for how to find a grid reference on a map).

PARK:
In the free marked car park, Old Quarry Gardens in the village just past the castle on the Mells road.

SETTING OFF:
Go right through an opening in the fence and cross the end of a hollow. Turn right on the path. Shortly, turn back left on a footpath, before reaching the road. Follow the path all the way to a gate into a field.

1. Field
Follow the path straight on (do not veer right). Here you start to see horse jumps for a cross country course. If there are horses using the course, take care and use your eyes and ears. Reach the far side. Up ahead in the hedge is a stile with upright post.

You return here later. But now, turn right keeping the pond on your right.

 Try making a grass whistle (Activity No. 8).

2. Sculptures
Reach a wooden duck and crocodile. These are very good examples of chain saw sculpture. Keep the bank on your left and continue all the way to the Nunney Brook.

3. Ford
Go through a kissing gate and over the bridge by the ford. Turn left along the brook.

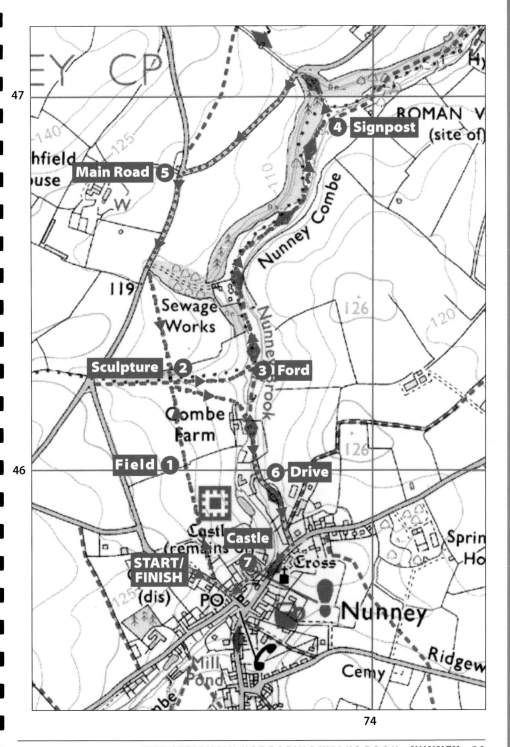

It's a good place to find sticks for a stick race (Activity No. 5).

Pass a small beach where you can paddle or begin your stick race.

 As you go along, look at the trees and see if you can see faces in them or special shapes.

You may see this fungus, commonly known as 'King Alfred's cakes'.

If you come in early spring you will be able to smell the wild garlic. The leaves are very tasty to eat in a salad or in cooking. Later there are bluebells and other wild flowers.

4. Signpost
Reach a signpost. Turn left across the bridge. The track climbs gently and leads to a lane. Turn left. It should be very quiet. At the top reach the main road.

5. Main Road
Turn left, walking along the grass verge. These next 3 or 4 minutes on the road need care. Lorries for the nearby quarry use the road. Pass a track and about 28 paces on, cross a stile on the left into a field.

Head straight across. There are two telegraph poles in the field. Aim for the right hand one. Continue to the stile with post in the hedge that you saw earlier.

Turn left, retracing your steps to the brook again. Cross and now turn right along the stream. Go through a kissing gate.

A kissing gate is not actually for kissing – although that is up to you! It is called that because the gate, as it swings, just lightly touches the frame – or 'kisses' it.

6. Drive
Follow the drive straight on under an avenue of trees.

Carry on in the same direction. You are now on Donkey Lane and this leads to the main village road. Turn right into Mells.

Pass an open area by the brook. Years ago when cloth was made in the village this was used as a place to wash wool.

You pass the church.

There are some interesting tombs and monuments in it… one is of Sir John who had the castle built.

7. Castle
Turn right over a footbridge and come to Nunney Castle. You can walk around the moat and explore the castle inside. There is an information board .

A *Think about:* What would life have been like here? Can you imagine arriving at the main door over the drawbridge? Where would you have eaten? And where would you have slept?

How many towers are there, how many floors? Can you spot the old kitchen fireplace, the toilets (garde robes) best seen on the outside of the towers? What happened to the castle in the Civil War?

After exploring, go straight ahead from the castle to a road in the village and turn right back to the quarry car park.

There is a shop in Nunney and a very popular family pub, the George.

✔ SPOT CHECK

Can you find this *thingy*?

Visit an old burial chamber

What's so good about it?

- Follow Wellow brook • See a pill box – what is it?
- Visit an old long barrow burial chamber
- Find a large ammonite • Cross a ford

Ⓐ Activities to enjoy:

- *Stick races on the stream*
- *Measure the height of a tree*
- *Use your imagination at the long barrow.*

What to take:

✔Rucksack; ✔light waterproof jacket; ✔good stout shoes or boots; ✔picnic or snacks; ✔water; ✔notebook and pen; ✔a camera.

START:

Wellow village. This is North East of Radstock. On the A367 roundabout by Peasedown St John, turn down the lane signed to Wellow. OS Explorer Map 142, grid ref. 738 581.

PARK:

In the free car park – near the centre of the village on the site of the old railway sidings

SETTING OFF:

Can you imagine it here when the railway was running? It was opened in 1874 with great celebration. The bells rang out from the village church for the first train. It carried goods and people to and from the village for over 90 years.

As you walk out of the car park, pass the old station building – now a house. Turn right at the road.

1. Pub

Reach the village centre and a pub, the Fox and Badger. Turn right down Railway Lane and come to the old Signal Box *(below)*. Go down the path at the side.

Half way down, cross a stile on the right. The path goes down to a garden and tennis court. Come close to the stream, the Wellow Brook. Go on a bit further and cross another

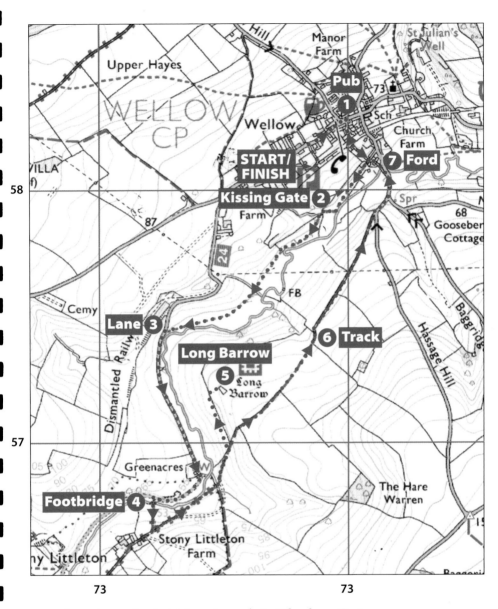

stile. Go through woodland with lots of different kinds of trees.

A *Can you identify any of them? There is cherry and silver birch for a start.*

Cross a small side stream.

1. Kissing Gate
Go through a kissing gate.

Go through an orchard of apples and pears.

A *These are not too high so why not try and measure the height of one of them (Activity No. 3).*

Come very close to the stream. This is where you can have a go at stick races. As you go on you can see that the stream is fast in some places and slow in others because it is is winding and there are shallow areas and large stones.

A *Stop for a moment and just listen to any sounds you can here. Can you hear the water, the wind, animals, birds or just silence?*

Over in the field on your right see a brick building with a tree growing out of it. This is a World War 2 pill box and would have been used by our home guard and soldiers if the Germans invaded.

This is was one of a line of pillboxes and concrete bollards put in to defend Bristol from the Germans and was finished by the summer of 1940 but two months later we had won the Battle of Britain and invasion was unlikely so they were never used.

Cross a stile and turn left on the lane.

2. Lane
Soon come to a small car park on the left. Go through it and cross a bridge over Wellow Brook.

A *This is a really good place to have a stick race from the bridge (Activity No. 5).*

A *Count the number of planks on the bridge. See answer on page 56.*

Go over a stile on the left. There is an 'Ancient Monument' sign. Then follow the hedge on your left and climb uphill. Look for a stile in the left hedge with a sign to the Long Barrow. Cross and go ahead with hedge on your right. Cross a stile on the right and go across and over another stile. You are now at the Stony Littleton Long Barrow.

2. Long Barrow
Thousands of years ago in Neolithic times this was a place where the early Britons worshipped and buried their dead. Look inside and see the chambers where the bodies were buried on each side.

On the left side of the entrance low down is a special fossil, placed here as it was thought to be really special. Was it seen as a stone serpent? On the right of the entrance see a number of other ancient fossils.

A *Use your pacing to see if you can measure the length of the barrow (Activity No. 10). Answer at the back of the book.*

Go back over the first stile and then turn left along the fence. Reach a stile ahead of you. Don't cross it. Stay in the field and turn left along the top. You can see the barrow over on the left.

Keep in this direction through a couple of

fields and join a track. Go straight along. Come to a lane and turn down hill. Keep round to the left and reach a very pretty ford with a flood level pole.

A *The water is clear and clean and it would be a good place for a paddle.*

Go to the end of the bridge and up the footpath which climbs up to the village. On the way pass the stile you crossed earlier. Retrace your steps.

Just on a little past the turning to the car park is the village shop. This is another community shop run by volunteers (like the one at Mells, Walk 9).

✔ SPOT CHECK

Can you find this *ammonite*?

Up the Gorge

What's so good about it?

- Two wonderful viewpoints over Somerset
- A 3m high cave bear • A scramble up Ebbor Gorge

Activities to enjoy:

- *Fly a kite*
- *Make a mini shelter*
- *Make a leaf rubbing*
- *Spot a kestrel and maybe a buzzard*

What to take:

✔Your kite; ✔rucksack; ✔waterproof jacket; ✔good stout shoes or boots; ✔a camera;
✔a book of trees; ✔sheets of kitchen roll and a flat book you can put the leaf in to rub at home;
✔a notebook and pen.

START:

At Deer Leap. This is about 1km from Priddy on the road leading to Wookey Hole, N West of Wells. OS map Explorer 141 Cheddar Gorge & Mendip Hills West 518 494 (see page 50 for how to find a grid reference on a map).

PARK:

At Deer Leap parking and picnic area.

SETTING OFF:

From Deer Leap there are widespread views over the Levels, and on a clear day see Glastonbury Tor and Brent Knoll. Imagine the scene thousands of years ago when it was flooded below and the hills were islands.

(A) *For a great place for kite flying, go through into the field at the side. This is owned by Somerset County Council who welcome visitors.*

To start the walk, go down through the picnic site and follow the grass path keeping the road on your left. At a field gate which is on your right, turn away from it to the left and cross the road.

1. Stile

Cross the stile.

Go right through two fields with a stile on the way and then another stile back onto the road. Turn left. On your right in the field see two standing stones. Legend has it that they were spaced just the distance apart that a hunted deer was said to have jumped. That's why this area is called Deer Leap.

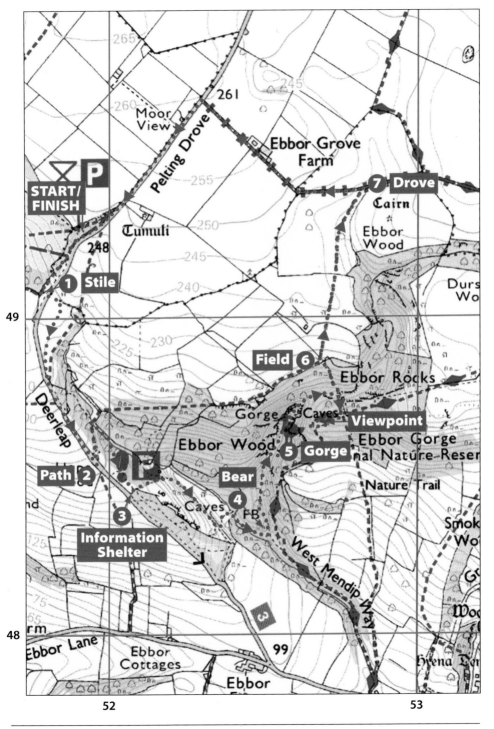

START/
FINISH

P

Moor
View

261

Pelting Drove

Ebbor Grove
Farm

7 Drove

Cairn

Ebbor
Wood

Durs
Wo

Tumuli

248

250

1 Stile

245

240

230

225

Field 6

Ebbor Rocks

Deerleap

Gorge

Caves

Viewpoint

Ebbor Gorge
nal Nature Reser

Ebbor Wood

5 Gorge

Path 2

P

Bear

Nature Trail

Smok
Wo

3

Caves

4

FB

Information
Shelter

West Mendip Way

Gr

3

Ebbor Lane

Ebbor
Cottages

99

Hyena

Ebbor

52

53

2. Path

Continue down the road for about 3 mins. Look out for a path on the left. Cross over a stile into Ebbor Gorge National Nature Reserve. The path goes away from the road. At a junction with another path, turn right and follow this. Then fork left and go along by railings with the gorge plunging down on the left.

3. Information Shelter

Reach an information shelter by a car park.

Ⓐ *Make sure you read this so you know some of the animals, birds, flowers and trees to look out for in the Gorge.*

Cross the stone stile left and go down steps into the deep wooded gorge. At a junction, turn left following the signs to the Gorge.

Come down into a wooded glade with a lot of hornbeam trees by a stream

Ⓐ *Their leaves would be good for a leaf rubbing at home. Choose one or two and pack them carefully flat between kitchen roll in your book. See Activity No. 4 on page 51, or find another kind of leaf as you go along.*

Ⓐ *This is also a good place for making a mini shelter (Activity No. 6).*

4. Bear

Look out for a giant bear sculpture on the left, quite a surprise.

*It was made from willow by sculptor **Sophie Courtier** and local schoolchildren to celebrate the 40th anniversary of Ebbor Gorge as a National Nature Resereve in June 2009. Bones of huge bears like this and other large, now extinct animals, were found in caves in the Gorge.*

Carry on to a junction and turn left towards the Gorge. You will soon start to climb and the path becomes rockier.

Ⓐ *Look for animal tracks and see if you can identify them from the footprints.*

5. Gorge

Then start your scramble up the Gorge.

Ⓐ *Use the 'three points of contact' rule so that you have contact with the ground and rocks in three places at all times – one hand, two feet, or two hands and one foot.*

Follow the path on and up to a junction. Now our walk takes us there and back to a viewpoint which is a good place for a picnic. For this, turn right up towards the car park. Go on a bit more and at a T-junction go right where there is a 'Caution Cliff' sign. This leads to a fabulous viewpoint high in the Gorge. Take care as this is a dangerous cliff edge and keep your dog on a lead. And don't fly your kite here.

A *It is a good place to spot a **kestrel** and the much larger **buzzard** flying and hovering above.*

Retrace your steps back to the junction and turn left back down to the second junction where you were before at the top of the gorge. Now continue straight on climbing up the small rocky path. It is quite steep and leads to a stile at the top into a field.

✔ SPOT CHECK

Can you find this *thingy*?

6. Field

Go up into the field and turn right over a stile. Go across to a stile on the far side. Go up a bank into the field and then straight across the flat to a stile. Once over this continue on keeping the hedge fairly close on the right. Near the corner, climb over a stile onto Dursdon Drove.

7. Drove

This is an ancient route across the Mendip Hills used for moving animals. It is now a BOAT – a Byway Open to All Traffic – so you may encounter a cyclist, or an off-road vehicle.

Turn left. Soon join a wider track and bear right on it. Follow it out past a farm to the Deer Leap Lane.

Turn left and after a few minutes reach the car park.

Activities

A 1. How to read a Grid Reference

Britain has been divided up into squares by the Ordinance Survey, who make our maps.

So if we want to find a place on a map, we can use a grid reference.

The numbers of the grid squares go up the sides and across the top and bottom.

1. Read across the bottom first. Then read up the side – an easy way to remember this is **along the corridor and up the stairs**.

2. **To give a simple 4 figure grid reference**, locate the place you want. Find the grid square it is in. Then write down the number of the square – go along the bottom first, **along the corridor**, and then go up the side, **up the stairs**, and write down that number. You now have two sets of numbers, e.g. 29 and 51. Your place is somewhere in that square which on the ground is a square kilometre. Look at *Fig. 1* to help you work it out.

3. To get closer to your place you need **a six number grid reference** which brings you to within 100m. For this, divide the square into sections of ten. As before, go across the bottom first and then up the side to where your place is. Then write down or read off the numbers that correspond to it, and add them onto the ends of your existing 2

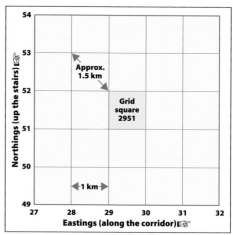

Fig. 1

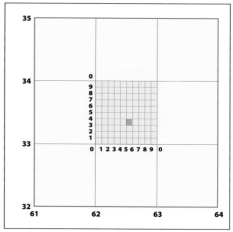

Fig. 2

sets of numbers, eg, 625 333. Take a look at *Fig. 2* this time to help you.

Ask your parent or an adult for help if you find this confusing.

A 2. How to find the age of a tree

Bring string, and a ruler or tape measure. You need two people for this. First of all measure from the base of the tree 1.5m up, and get your helper to mark the spot. Next run the string around the outside of the tree trunk, but try to avoid a spot where there are bulges or lumps. You have now measured the circumference of the tree, which you will need to divide by 2.5cm. This means that for every 2.5cm your tree is one year old. Although this is not completely accurate it will give you an idea of the tree's age. By counting backwards you can work out the date when it started to grow. What was happening in history at that time?

3. How to measure the height of a tree

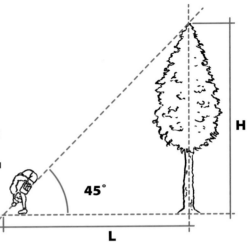

Bring string and a ruler or a tape measure. This is fun and very simple! The ground must be flat around the tree you have chosen – not sloping. Walk away from the tree with your back to it. At intervals bend down and look between your legs. Stop when you can just see the top of the tree, and measure the distance along the ground to the base of the tree. You could use your pacing for this or a tape measure. When you bend down and look between your legs you are looking up at an angle of 45° and making a triangle so the distance along the ground to the base of the tree is the same as the height of the tree.

4. Leaf rubbing

You will need:

At home: Some plain white thin paper, a wax crayon

On the walk: Take a book and some kitchen roll so you can keep the leaf flat until you get home.

Choose a leaf with fairly pronounced veins on the back. I chose a cob nut leaf. Oak is good, and beech and also wych elm. Try a few and see how you get on.

When you get home, put the leaf flat on a hard surface and lay the sheet of paper on top. Press down gently, so the leaf is flat and you can just start to see the shape underneath. Hold it firmly and with the wax crayon rub gently over the leaf, trying not to go over the edges. Try different techniques – rubbing in one direction and keeping an even pressure is good. Don't push the tip of the crayon into the paper. You will find the best way with practice.

Then, hey presto! You have your leaf as a record. Write down the name of the leaf and on which walk you found it.

5. Racing Sticks

Here's a game for river or stream, that has all the thrill of a real boat race!

Each person chooses a stick. Try and make sure that they are all the same size, and mark your sticks so they can be easily seen and you know which belongs to each person.

Then choose a start point, and just as important a finish line. All the sticks must go into the water at the same time and place and the water flow will do the rest! Some will get stuck on stones, others may be swept into a side pool, but the winner is the first stick across the line! The only rule is the sticks must be dead or fallen, never break a tree or bush to get them.

A 6. Mini shelter building

Could you survive if you were 10cm tall? This is all about design and building that is only limited by your imagination!

Building a mini shelter to house 'very tiny people' is great fun, and you don't need any experience.

Collect plenty of dead sticks and find a suitable area, perhaps in woodland or a clearing, and let you imagination do the rest! Or make a stone shelter by collecting different pebbles and stones and combine sticks or feathers or seaweed – whatever is there to use.

Here are a couple of ideas we had, but you will soon work out better ones.

The only rule is don't pick or break off any living plants or branches. Only use dead or fallen sticks. Leave your shelter when it is finished. You never know what small creatures may use your little house!

A 7. Compass in a puddle

Here is a very simple compass that you can easily make and use in a puddle or cup of water. You will need:

- A paper clip
- Magnet (a fridge magnet will do)
- Leaf

First undo the paper clip until you have just the small loop at the end, you can use this as a handle later. Next magnetise the opened end of the paper clip by rubbing the magnet down it in one direction. Once it has been magnetised, thread it through your leaf down the centre rib, and gently place it on the water. Watch as it turns the magnetised end of the paper clip towards north.

A 8. How to make a grass whistle

This is great fun, and so easy! Find a wide blade of grass. Hold your hands together with your thumbs pointing back towards you and your fingers in the air, much like you would for a prayer. Trap the blade of grass between your thumbs , and the fleshy part at the base of your thumbs. Make sure

it's taut, and blow hard on the leaf edge which is held tight between your thumbs. With a little practice you can make an interesting noise, and it is different every time!

9. How to track

Early man moved about the forests and land in search of food. So that their family could follow them, they left signals to mark their trail.

Why don't you and your family try this. One of the ways to show the trail is with an arrow or sticks or stones on the ground pointing in the direction you are going. Place these at places where you have to change direction, like a junction, and confirm this direction soon with another arrow. Then those who follow know they are on the right track. You can put a cross of sticks to show 'no entry'.

Learn to recognise animal tracks in the ground. They will tell you a lot about who, and what has been there before you.

10. Pacing and steps

PACING – It is useful to know the length of your pace – the distance from the back of the heel on your back foot to the front of your boot on the front foot. This means you can measure distances without a tape measure.

To find you pace, measure out 100m and walk it in a natural way – not big or smaller steps than usual. Count the number of steps. If it is, say, 70 then you know that for every 70 paces you walk about 100m.

FOOT LENGTH – Also useful to know the length of your foot in boot or trainer. Measure it and if you need to mark out a distance just put one foot in front of the other, heel touching toe. Count the number of steps and multiply by the length of your boot. If the boot is 25cm and you take five steps, then you have measured 125cm.

11. Sticky stones

A bit of fun!

Find three stones of about 25-30cm across. Ask your friend or parent to press two of them together hard for the count of 30 using mainly the tips of fingers. It can be tiring!

Meanwhile you take the other stone and make small circles around their hands almost like the moon orbiting the planet. It needs to be up and down, not side to side, and maybe you say a few 'magic words'.

At the end ask the person to gently try and prise the stones apart. They should find it quite hard, as though the stones are held together by some special force.

A 12. Diamond Kite

It's good fun and quite magical to watch your kite dancing in the sky. You can of course buy one very cheaply, but it's even better to make your own. Here is a very simple design which flies well!

You will need:

- Thin coloured plastic – old carrier bags. A bright colour shows up best in the sky
- 2 wooden thin sticks of the same length such as bamboo BBQ skewers or thin wooden sticks about 30-45cm long or longer
- Clear sticky tape – scotch tape or packing tape
- About 16m of thin string or very strong sewing thread
- Ruler, marker pen, scissors (big enough to cut stick)
- A flat space

1. If using bamboo skewers, snip off the points.
2. Mark the centre of both sticks. Then on one stick make another mark half way between the centre and one end (a quarter) *Diagram A*.
3. Flatten the single sheet of plastic. Arrange the sticks in a cross. One stick's halfway mark crosses the other stick's quarter mark. You can use a ruler to make sure the sticks cross at right angles.
4. Mark the position of stick ends with clear dots from your marker *Diagram B*.
5. Remove the sticks and connect dots into a diamond shape using ruler. Cut out the shape *Diagram C*.
6. Put the sticks back on. Stretch the plastic so it is flat and quite tight. Secure the ends with short pieces of tape. Put half of the tape underneath the plastic and then wrap over onto the stick end on top of plastic *Diagram D*.
7. **Tail:** It is very important and must be at least 10 times the length of your kite. It gives the kite balance and keeps it pointing up. Cut out ribbons of plastic from the bags, about 40cm wide and 10 times the length of kite. Use a simple knot to tie the pieces together. They don't have to be the same length. Thread one end of the tail between the vertical stick and the plastic, at the bottom of the kite above the tape and tie *Diagram E*.
8. **String:** Turn the kite over. Where the sticks cross, make two small holes in the plastic

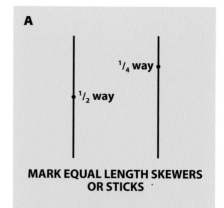

A

¹/₄ **way**

¹/₂ **way**

MARK EQUAL LENGTH SKEWERS OR STICKS

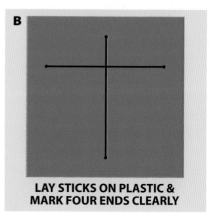

B

LAY STICKS ON PLASTIC & MARK FOUR ENDS CLEARLY

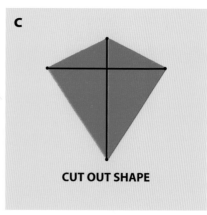

C

CUT OUT SHAPE

using a tack, pencil point or needle. The holes are diagonal to each other each side of the crossed sticks. Poke the kite string through one hole. Loop it over both sticks and poke it through the other diagonal hole and tie together with a good knot *Diagram E*.

Wind the string around a piece of wood or unsharpened pencil to make a spool. Tie the string to the spool or it may escape!

9. Find an open area with wind and you are ready to go.

Safety! Don't fly the kite near electric power cables or in a thunderstorm.

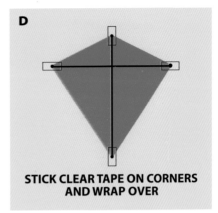

STICK CLEAR TAPE ON CORNERS AND WRAP OVER

13. Ley line Hunting

Science has proven the existence of **ley lines**, (lines of earth energy) and shown that many of the ancient monuments like the Stanton Drew Stone Circles are positioned on them. So why not try your hand at dowsing, and go hunting maybe for a ley line on Walk 7 on page 26. Dowsing has been around for thousands of years, and is still used to find underground energies, water, metal objects and who knows what else.

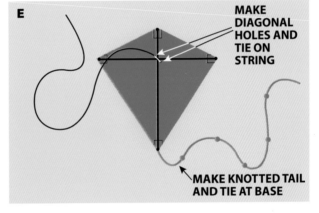

MAKE DIAGONAL HOLES AND TIE ON STRING

MAKE KNOTTED TAIL AND TIE AT BASE

To make simple dowsing rods, take two metal coat hangers about 37.5cm long. Bend 15cm at the ends into an 'L' shape that will give you two handles to hold, and put them into a couple of empty ball point pen tubes. Even simple angle rods like these can be very sensitive.

To go dowsing, hold your rods, one in each hand, at waist height with your elbows tucked into your sides.

Walk slowly with the tips of the rods slightly down from the horizontal, and ask the rods "to find the energy" emitted from the standing stones or ley lines.

You will find that the tips will swing gently and may get as far as crossing over in front of you.

You have probably found a ley line, or some other mystery object beneath the surface. Turn at right angles to you path, and the rods should point straight ahead again. If you wander off the line, they will cross over, telling you to come back.

Why not try it? It's fun. Although it may not work for everyone, it's worth having a go! It worked for us at the Stone Circles!

SPOT CHECK

ANSWERS

Walk 1 • Middle Hope
Ordnance Survey plaque on trig point

Walk 2 • Winscombe
Metal arched vehicle barrier

Walk 3 • Rowberrow
Doggy flap gate

Walk 4 • Burrington
Sign for bridleway and a circular walking route on pole

Walk 5 • Blagdon
Top of ventilation shaft for an underground pipe

Walk 6 • Chew
One of the illustrated number posts on Grebe Trail

Walk 7 • Stanton Drew
Arch over a stream

Walk 8 • Kilmersdon
A slate drawing of the nursery rhyme character

Walk 9 • Mells
St George statue on top of war memorial

Walk 10 • Nunney
Garde robe (toilet) on Nunney Castle tower

Walk 11 • Wellow
The fossil of an ammonite

Walk 12 • Ebbor
Fishing float, now topping a gate post

Answers to questions on the Walks

Walk 2 (p. 8)
- The trees are, from top to bottom: ash, hazel, field maple
- Shute Shelve Tunnel is 200m long

Walk 4 (p. 14)
- A yellow arrow shows a footpath for walkers, and a blue arrow shows a bridleway for horse riders. See if you can find out how these paths are shown on an Ordnance Survey map.

Walk 5 (p. 18)
- Number of planks: 60

Walk 7 (p. 27)
- There are 16 arches in the viaduct

Walk 9 (p. 34 & p. 37)
- A Talbot was large white hunting dog. Sadly, there are no more left. The dog is often shown on Coats of Arms.
- The telegraph poles are 100 metres apart

Walk 11 (p. 44)
- There are 57 planks on the bridge
- The long barrow is 30m long